MOOCs

What Every ESL Teacher Needs to Know

Pamela S. H. Bogart

University of Michigan Press
Ann Arbor

First paperback edition 2023

Published in the United States of America by the
University of Michigan Press

First published January 2019

The presentation of tables, figures, and/or images is dependent on the device and display options. Some image content or language characters may have been removed or may be altered depending on the device used to read this ebook.

Paperback ISBN: 978-0-472-03944-9
Ebook ISBN: 978-0-472-12562-3

MOOCs

ACKNOWLEDGMENTS

Many thanks to the extraordinary community of educators who contributed to this endeavor. At the University of Michigan, my guide and editor, Kelly Sippell, director of the English Language Institute; Angelo Pitillo at the Language Resource Center; Philomena Meechan, the incredible team at Academic Innovation, in particular Bryon Maxey, Scott Mahler, Rebecca Quintana, and Steven Welsch; and at the Center for Research on Learning and Teaching, Tracy Bartholomew. Thank you to Handi Kurniawan, who demonstrated how to promote a vibrant learning community as course assistant in the first MOOC I created. Thank you to my dear friend and collaborator, India Plough at Michigan State University, for generously sharing her wisdom. Finally, an enthusiastic thank-you to the graduate students in the MOOC *Preparing for Graduate Study in the U.S.* and our local online course *Preparing for Graduate Success*, who helped to shape what dynamic online learning can become.

ABOUT THE AUTHOR

Pamela S. H. Bogart teaches academic and professional English communication courses to graduate students, and language teacher preparation courses to undergraduates at the University of Michigan English Language Institute. After teaching English internationally and earning her MA in French at the University of Michigan in 1994, she led adult and family literacy and ESL programs in the community. In 2000, she returned to the University of Michigan to teach both French and English for international students, earning her MA in TESOL at Eastern Michigan University in 2003, and turning to full-time curriculum development, program coordination, teaching, and digital initiatives at the English Language Institute. Pamela's approach to language teaching emphasizes learner self-efficacy, language use in social context, personalization of learning, and fostering supportive learning communities.

CONTENTS

Introduction

Back in 2012, the *New York Times* ran a story about MOOCs, entitled "Instruction for Masses Knocks Down Campus Walls" (Lewin, 2012). Well, the campus walls still exist, but MOOCs, or **massive open online courses**, have made the walls a little bit more permeable to the general public. MOOCs are hot topics at professional conferences and in teacher education programs. The proliferation of language-learning MOOCs is evident. A September 2018 search of ClassCentral.com yields 100 currently running communication skills MOOCs, for both first-language and additional-language learners. MOOCs offer (at least some) free content, are time-flexible and low stakes, and can be an engaging way to build knowledge and skills, including language skills.

The campus where I teach, the University of Michigan, has encouraged faculty to experiment with this new mode of teaching and learning beyond traditional classroom boundaries. As an avid proponent of equipping students to extend their language learning autonomously, I was optimistic about the potential language-learning benefits of MOOCs. This book is an exploration of that optimism. From my perspective as a teacher of English and French as additional languages in school, community, and university settings since 1985, I'll offer a response to three questions that address why and how MOOCs are relevant to ESL and EFL teachers.

1. What is a MOOC?
2. How can my ESL students best use MOOCs?
3. What if I were asked or decided to create a MOOC?

At the end of each discussion, readers will find Exploration tasks that can serve as a bridge between this book and some hands-on MOOC experiences and increase readers' knowledge of and familiarity with MOOCs.

Who Is This Book For?

This book is written for English language teachers who work with multilingual adults or children over the age of 10. While MOOCs are typically designed for grown-ups, they can be a useful learning supplement for tweens and teens as well. Teachers may be in a variety of settings worldwide—ESL (English as a Second Language), EFL (English as a Foreign Language), EAL (English as an Additional Language), EAP (English for Academic Purposes), ESP (English for Specific Purposes), or in bilingual programs. This book will use the term *ESL* as a shorthand to encompass all of these teaching contexts.

Why might ESL teachers in particular want to know more about MOOCs? First, MOOCs can be a free language-learning resource. The MOOC universe, however, can be a little bit bewildering to navigate. Scaffolding by an ESL teacher may help provide a smoother entry, and a means for a teacher to provide differentiated instruction to learners with varying goals, capabilities, and needs. Second, instructors on most college campuses keep hearing about MOOCs and may even be asked to develop one.

Enrolling in a few MOOCs is one of the best ways to prepare to wrap your mind around the possibilities before referring students to MOOCs or designing a MOOC yourself. At the University of Michigan English Language Institute, I do all three: enrolling as a student in MOOCs, referring students to MOOCs, and creating new MOOCs. A little bit of context: I teach English for academic and professional communication. My students, from across the globe, are enrolled in graduate degree programs on our campus. To help new students prepare for the transition to these graduate programs at Michigan, we started looking at designing an online pre-arrival option. Building a MOOC seemed to be just the thing—massive, open, and online, easy to access anytime, from anywhere in the world. The MOOC creation process helped me to digest how needs assessment, curriculum design, and teacher–learner interactions differ in MOOCs compared to more traditional learning environments, even "traditional" *online* environments. As I share my story with you, we'll look at these unique features of MOOCs among online courses, and the relevance of MOOCs to ESL teaching in secondary, university, community, and professional contexts.

Question 1
What Is a MOOC?

A **MOOC** (a massive open online course) is a particular model of internet-based learning: **m**assive, in that the courses are designed for thousands to participate simultaneously; **o**pen, available to any individual learner who wishes to register (and initially free); **o**nline, existing only on a web platform with no campus location; and a **c**ourse, typically a three- to six-week set of lessons with lectures, exercises, tests, and grades. This set of lessons typically restarts with a new "welcome mat" every few weeks, so entry and re-entry are possible at multiple times over any given year. MOOCs generally do not hold class at specific times; rather, students can take advantage of recorded video lectures, discussion forums, tasks, and assessments on their own schedule.

What does *massive* really mean in the MOOC context? MOOC platforms are equipped to handle thousands of self-registering learners at once. In practice, a particular MOOC may have 2,000–3,000 learners at one time, or it may be tiny, with just two or three learners actively participating in a given cohort of several hundred enrolled. The tens, hundreds, or thousands who participate are often living across the globe, transforming traditional campus boundaries to open, shared learning and extending participation to every person with access to the internet and adequate bandwidth to stream video. In this book, I'll focus mainly on the truly *open* MOOCs where students can sign up to audit the course for free, have access to at least a portion of course materials, and may roll over enrollment from one class session to the next, floating between cohorts and participating in MOOC coursework as time allows.

It's important to also state what MOOCs are not. It's possible to liken MOOCs to a YouTube instructional channel or a Khan Academy lesson sequence, but MOOCs are not identical to these alternate online resources. Like YouTube, video is typically a main source of content in MOOCs, but there are also discussion forums, assignments, and quizzes. These assignment types are designed to help students remember, practice, and demonstrate what they learned in the video content. The opportunity to pose and answer questions with and for classmates in discussion forums makes MOOCs a slightly different animal from an individual instructional platform like Khan Academy, in which learning is a solitary process. Khan Academy is one educational provider with a consistent approach to pedagogy, whereas the universe of MOOCs offers access to hundreds of institutions and instructional approaches.

Brief History

This section is labeled "brief" because there is only about a decade of history to tell. The first massive open online course, based at the University of Manitoba (Canada), enrolled more than 2,300 learners in dynamic global collaboration in 2008 (Yeager, Hurley-Dasgupta, & Bliss, 2013). The first lecture-based MOOCs from big-name U.S. universities emerged on the scene in 2012 and 2013. The word *MOOC* appeared in only 10 words per billion in the "News of the World" (NOW) corpus in 2011, surging to 1,730 words per billion by 2013 (http://corpus.byu.edu/now).

Why are MOOCs such a big deal? In that first big wave of MOOCs, news coverage portended the end of expensive college education as we know it, the dissolution of colleges and universities, and a free elite education accessible to all. Today, as the MOOC landscape has matured, the hype has receded (reaching a pretty stable 150 words per billion in 2016 and 2017 in the NOW corpus). Educational institutions still thrive. Rather than competing with MOOCs for students, colleges and universities host the majority of MOOCs for complementary and overlapping purposes that include outreach, public service, lifelong learning, supplementary learning materials, and marketing/promotion.

An important element of university public service is to disseminate new knowledge. MOOCs permit schools to share the latest expertise on topics such as environmental stewardship or a healthy diet. Given the wide range of academic background, life experience, skills, and outlooks that students bring to any campus, most institutions make an effort to provide support to students regarding the academic and life skills that will enable them to thrive. MOOCs are now part of that menu of support options. In other words, MOOCs can help students become better prepared before they arrive, rather than waiting for support to start after getting situated on campus. The relevance of MOOCs is not limited to this pre-campus phase of life, of course. MOOCs also provide a mechanism for institutions to connect with alumni to offer lifelong learning. *Open* means that everyone can theoretically also explore lifelong learning interests in MOOCs. Nevertheless, most MOOC learners already have at least a college degree or are in the process of earning one.

Marketing and promoting an institution by providing limited access to star faculty is a feature of many MOOCs. If a university has a strong intensive English face-to-face program, for example, the institution could promote that program by featuring its faculty members in instructional videos in a MOOC. Universities offer a certificate (for a fee) to students who complete their MOOCs, another marketing element, but also something that potentially adds value to someone's career. A certificate of completion may aid job-seekers or document ongoing professional development to one's current employer. Many universities also now offer a "specialization," a series of four to six MOOCs on a given topic, such as "academic writing" or "data science." Some courses even translate into real college credit or contribute toward a "micro-masters" certification. These options require students to pay, but not as much as regular campus tuition—more like the price of a hefty textbook.

While content and platform options have expanded dramatically, open access options are now more constrained. Fee structures vary and are continually changing. Common schemes require payment to access the full array of course materials, to earn a certificate of completion, or to stay in the course for more than a short trial period. Like much new technology, MOOCs were built and popularized first for free, and then educational institutions and host platforms started to work on how to "monetize" or generate funding to support them.

A variety of types of MOOCs have emerged as a result. Almost all involve video streaming and enroll a tremendously international group of learners. A few MOOCs are designed by institutions to roll out professional development or transition training to their own students or employees, who may participate in private cohorts. Such MOOCs may also permit open enrollment by anyone interested. Some MOOCs encourage students to join the course with a group of colleagues, classmates, or friends, or to use the course discussion boards to formulate a group to foster a collaborative small team learning experience.

Subjects addressed in MOOCs vary widely. In the early days, computer programming and related fields represented the lion's share of offerings, but as of the writing of this book, the range of MOOC topics encompasses virtually every field imaginable. I find the list available at https://www.classcentral.com/subjects quite helpful when hunting for MOOCs. In terms of scope, I see quite a few courses that provide an introduction to the fundamentals of a topic, such as "Introduction to Marketing" or "Creative Writing," and another large collection with a narrow, specialized focus, such as "Identifying Food Fraud" or "Storytelling for Change." Those MOOCs that focus on niche technical skills are likely to attract specialists in particular fields while those that focus on introductory academic content, self-improvement, or extracurricular interests tend to attract a much broader array of participants.

Pedagogical Approaches

With the exception of **cMOOCs** (constructivist MOOCs), which involve the collaboration of a community of co-learners (Yeager, Hurley-Dasgupta, & Bliss, 2013), most early MOOCs sought to capitalize on the traditional university practice of student attendance at a large lecture. These **xMOOCs**, online versions of lecture-based courses, complement video-recorded lectures with comprehension-check quizzes and discussion boards. In other words, video micro-lectures and quizzes serve as the primary tools of learning, with discussion threads available for participants to try to clarify material. This structure would support a grammar-translation method of teaching and learning language or some structural drills, but not anything particularly communicative. These structural constraints make lecture-based MOOCs a less-than-ideal space for language learning. As the mode of instructional delivery matures, however, we can see more use of social media and collaborative tasks in the MOOC landscape even in xMOOCs. These changes offer new potential for interaction and communicative language use.

Interaction in xMOOCs vs. cMOOCs

The role of an instructor is often quite different in MOOCs as compared to more traditional online courses. As illustrated in Figure 1, on a continuum of "no ongoing instructor involvement" to high "interactive instructor involvement," xMOOCs tend toward the left, and small, for-credit online courses tend toward the right.

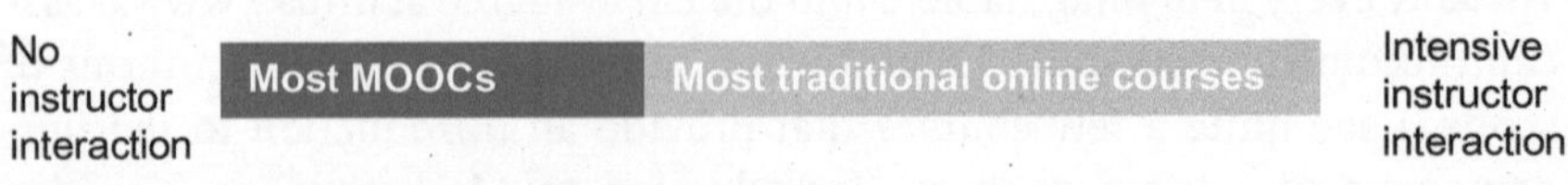

Figure 1: Degree of instructor interaction

Whereas instructors are usually paid to teach each iteration of a traditional online course (and are expected to interact with their students), in MOOCs, in contrast, instructors are generally not paid to stay involved with the MOOC after it launches. Monitoring of student participation in a MOOC may be minimal.

In the early planning stages of my first MOOC, this teacherless approach puzzled me. Given that extensive research into online learning demonstrates repeatedly that "teacher presence" positively impacts student participation and learning (e.g., Murphy, 2015), how can one create "teacher presence" without interacting with students enrolled in the MOOC? Our institutional design team provided valuable mentoring to me about this new pedagogical context. My guides explained that teacher presence is pre-populated (1) in videos, (2) in automated quiz feedback scripted to be as friendly and as personalized as possible, and (3) in weekly email missives scheduled to go out to each cohort automatically. These emails can be scripted by the lead teacher(s) in the course or by the institutional design and production team. In addition, course assistants, like TAs, may monitor forums for opportunities to encourage students and to respond to questions that classmates haven't answered. These course assistants may be paid, or they may be volunteers who are enthusiastic alumni of the course. Either way, the course assistants may respond to the concerns of individual students, filling one small slice of the traditional active teacher role.

We know that students need to use language to build proficiency. To what extent do MOOCs enable meaningful language use? Table 1 classifies MOOCs based on degree of interaction with not only the teacher (as shown in Figure 1), but also with course materials and classmates.

Not surprisingly, I would argue that the more a MOOC tends toward the right and more interactive side of the table, the more likely that MOOC is to promote language learning. MOOCs are not publicly listed by degree of interactivity on their host platforms or on aggregator sites, so figuring out what types of language learning are possible in a MOOC requires some advance exploration. Most MOOCs supply a syllabus on the pre-enrollment course information page, and the syllabus will often provide not only the sequence of topics but the kinds of assignments and the kinds of participation expected of students. This information can then be interpreted to predict the degree of communicative interactivity of a MOOC.

In xMOOCs, the predominant model, students learn content from videos and readings, use discussion forums to seek clarification from peers and course assistants, and practice using new knowledge and skills to complete

Table 1: MOOCs classified by degree and type of interaction

	not interactive ⟷ very interactive		
	xMOOCs		*cMOOCs*
	Information-provision MOOCs	**Interactive MOOCs**	**Constructivist MOOCs**
Interaction type	Lecture listening Recall quizzes Application activities	Extensive use of discussion forums for peer interaction Possible additional interaction in social media add-ons Possible small group tasks	Student collaboration to construct the knowledge generated by and learned in the MOOC
Parallel language teaching pedagogies	Grammar-translation Audio-lingual	Communicative approaches with teacher-as-expert, including content-based learning and task-based learning	Task-based learning Critical pedagogies Communicative approaches with teacher-as-facilitator and teacher-as-co-learner
Examples of what students do with language in this kind of MOOC	Listen Watch Read Observe Repeat Memorize Reproduce Pose written questions	Listen Watch Read Pose written questions Generate own ideas and communicate them in writing Navigate group work Fill out peer review rubrics View evaluative rubrics from peers Communicate off-platform with classmates (e.g., Facebook, WeChat, WhatsApp, Skype)	Listen Watch Read Pose written questions Generate own ideas and communicate them in writing Navigate group work Fill out peer review rubrics View evaluative rubrics from peers Communicate off-platform with classmates (e.g., Facebook, WeChat, WhatsApp, Skype) Collaborate to generate course content

Example activity types	Explanatory videos Scripted demo videos Multiple-choice quizzes Fill-in-the-blank quizzes Discussion forums for posing questions about concepts *If a MOOC for language learning:* • Scripted dialogues for memorization • Vocabulary flashcards • Form-focused grammar exercises	Explanatory videos Authentic language video samples Open-ended discussion questions Revising writing in response to peer-graded tasks *If a MOOC for language learning:* • Form, meaning, and use-focused grammar exercises • Group projects to practice a language function or in a target language context • Supplementary social media communicative practice	Thought-provoking dramatized or authentic video clips Autoethnographic projects Reflections on learning tasks Group tasks (often supported on a 3rd-party platform or on social media) Research on content, data, theory to contribute to the class content Contributing own expertise Collaborative real-world problem-solving *If a MOOC for language learning:* • Form, meaning, and use-focused grammar investigation, reflection, and peer teaching • Group projects to investigate and teach a language function in a target language context • Supplementary social media communicative practice
Example MOOCs	Artificial Intelligence for Robotics (Stanford University, on Udacity) Guitar for Beginners (Berklee College of Music, on Coursera)	English Grammar and Essay Writing (Berkeley, on EdX) Social Media (Instructure, on Canvas Network)	cMALT (Certified Member of the Association for Learning Technologies) cMOOC (a combination of social media platforms)

tasks and quizzes. There may be thousands of students enrolled, so only a small proportion of students are likely to interact with a course assistant. Discussion boards tend to consist of hundreds of individual posts, most without replies.

The typical xMOOC, therefore, is not ideal for promoting language learning. Nonetheless, seen as a supplement to other forums for more communicative language learning, an xMOOC does still offer some special value. Language learning can be enhanced through the ways in which online environments allow for extensive authentic language input. Students can digest lots of audio and video on demand and, unlike YouTube, a MOOC can frame that media content with strategic suggestions on how to consume it. Some of the explanatory video footage in xMOOCs is beautifully crafted and is rich in visual support through animations, diagrams, demonstrations, and more. MOOC students can also practice reading in MOOC assignments and discussion boards.

Given the reliance by many MOOCs on discussion boards as the only potential interactive space, an xMOOC student can practice articulating thoughts in writing by initiating discussion board posts. There is no guarantee that anyone will actually write back. Even without replies, this practice will require lots of composition of meaningful communication with attention to politeness strategies and clear wording. Students are likely to use the genre of written posts to online discussions even in face-to-face courses, which involve online discussions in growing numbers. Online discussion posts share certain conventions with email, another type of writing that students will do in the target language in both school and work settings. Thus computer-mediated written communication is a skill that students can practice extensively in a MOOC. Feedback and interaction with an instructor or interaction with peers around the writing process, however, would typically be lacking in an xMOOC. Even though peer grading with a simple rubric may be a required "peer review" component of the course, rubrics are often set up just to assign points, not to prompt extended feedback or interaction.

The middle column of Table 1 characterizes some xMOOCs as more interactive. These MOOCs may encourage responses to peer posts on discussion boards or invite students to gather via social media off the MOOC platform for text-, audio-, and video-based discussion. Such xMOOCs may be well-suited to a student's language-learning goals. An xMOOC can also point students to additional digital tools for language learning, such as adaptive reading comprehension assessment to provide texts appropriate for each student's proficiency level, or how-tos on investigating patterns of language use in online corpora. A variety of new technologies are being developed to try to substitute for a teacher's expertise, such as a grammar-checker integrated right into online learning platforms. I do not see this type of resource as a promising solution to the absence of an interactive teacher. For the time being, such tools treat writing more like following a recipe and less like the complex cognitive and social use of language that ESL teachers know written communication to be.

Nonetheless, the large size of xMOOCs can be an advantage. Those MOOCs that attract hundreds of learners at once can use crowdsourcing to generate multiple perspectives based on input from learners all over the world. In other words, hundreds of learners can supply hundreds of data points to inform the answer to a pertinent question. In our MOOC on preparing for graduate study in the U.S., for example, we ask students to find video footage of graduate students talking about their experiences at a campus they are planning or hoping to attend in the future, and then to frame and respond to this new video content with MOOC classmates in a discussion forum.

A contrasting model is that of the cMOOC. Online student participants collaborate with one another and with the instructor(s) to co-create the bulk of the course content. The cMOOC capitalizes on peer communication and connection to students' lives and careers, which can engage students in more authentic communication tasks and provide more authentic input. **Social constructivism**, an approach developed on the basis of Lev Vygotsky's groundbreaking psychological theory in the early 20th century (see Vygotsky, 1978), is a well-elaborated approach to education, but the term is not so widely used in describing language pedagogies. We hear more in language teacher training about the Vygotskian concept of the **zone of proximal development**, or the "can't-quite-do-it-myself-but-can-with-scaffolding" sweet spot where tutored language learning is believed to occur. There is nonetheless a great deal of overlap between, on one hand, Vygotsky's insistence that cognition develops through the process of situated social interaction and, on the other hand, interactionist, communicative theories of language teaching.

Ensuring that the cMOOC learning process be collaborative requires the MOOC teaching and design team to establish and offer three dimensions of online presence: **social presence**, which is about relationship-building, community-building, and identity; **cognitive presence**, which means introducing puzzles and highlighting problems and solutions raised by learners; and **teaching presence**, which means setting up the course objectives, tasks, and interface, facilitating effective student discussions and participating in these tasks with learners (Murphy, 2015). A cMOOC could provide language scaffolding for thematic domains or skill objectives, for example, and learners could contribute their knowledge, expertise, research, or experience to construct the course content together with the active participation of one or more instructors.

The cMOOC approach aligns well with socially contextualized pedagogies. Parallel to the popularization of communicative language teaching, community and adult educators in particular have advocated for an engaged approach grounded in the work of Paulo Freire (1970) in Brazil, where the purpose and process of education, particularly literacy development, challenge top-down educational and social structures. The problem-posing and collective problem-solving central to Freire's practice would suit a cMOOC, if students had access to the technology and computer literacy to participate. In the 21st century, a greater awareness of context, identity, and power are also evident in critical pedagogies. Critical pedagogies move beyond questions of how to accurately express one's ideas in a social context on to recognizing, navigating, and potentially shifting power relations that are expressed and constructed through language use in a social context. These kinds of approaches to language learning could be supported well in a cMOOC environment. At present, I have not seen this potential fully realized.

This constructivist participation in social, cognitive, and teaching dimensions requires significant ongoing involvement by a teacher-facilitator. MOOCs do not usually generate enough funding to pay that teacher's salary. The predominant xMOOC model assumes a teacher with a typical full-time load who records a few lectures and shares course objectives, materials, and sequence adapted from an existing face-to-face course. With that, a MOOC design team sets up online access to learners worldwide on a MOOC platform. As a result of this business model, xMOOCs are much more common than cMOOCs.

Assessment in MOOCs

One key feature and constraint on MOOC platforms is how students are graded: with an assumption that thousands may be participating, almost all student involvement is set up to be graded by machine, the individual students themselves, or peers. A lead teacher or teaching team generally doesn't need to do any grading. Again, this level of machine automation can be tricky to use for effective language learning, particularly since MOOC platforms aren't (yet) built to use today's speech-related technologies to handle oral assignments or text analysis algorithms to interact with or provide quality feedback on written submissions. Mistakes or errors on quizzes or exercises will usually either generate private automated feedback just to the student. (A MOOC teacher doesn't have access to a traditional gradebook.) Many graded exercises and assessments are set up to be available to do repeatedly, until a passing score is reached. Language and usage errors typically go unnoticed in discussion forums. There is a greater emphasis on listening, reading, and producing language than on exposure to accurate input during interaction.

Over time, MOOC platforms have begun developing more robust assignment, peer review, and rubric self-evaluation mechanisms, as well as starting to improve discussion thread interfaces. The range of content, pedagogical philosophies, and sponsoring institutions has blossomed. The increasing array of tools for analyzing big data means that MOOC providers are dipping a toe in the water and developing more potential resources for adaptive course design, where difficulty level or topic is adjusted for each learner based on their ongoing course performance. There are now dozens of popular language-learning MOOCs, with elements of grammar-translation, audio-lingual, and also more communicative task-based and content-based approaches. The timeline for this evolution is less than a decade, so as language teachers, we still have the opportunity to shape an ever-evolving type of learning platform to further improve its potential for language learning. How well are MOOCs realizing this potential to support language learning? Teachers who point students to MOOCs for supplementary learning will constantly need to shift footing, as the MOOC terrain continues to evolve (Gardner & Miller, 2014).

Exploration 1: Try One!

Sign up for a foreign or second-language MOOC on at least two different educational platforms. Do some Week 1 activities in each course and try to do some activities on a mobile device/tablet and some on a computer. Consider your own behaviors and reactions. What appeals to you and what annoys you on each platform? What engages you in each course? What helps you learn?

Here are five suggested platforms:

Canvas Network
Coursera
EdX
FutureLearn
Udacity

Consider enrolling in a course on a language you know well, so that you can expertly assess how the language is introduced in the MOOC. Try enrolling in another course on a language that is new to you, so that you can experience a novice introduction to that language within the MOOC environment. Even if the courses you sign up for aren't quite appropriate for your proficiency level, you should still be able to use them for the specific purpose here: to explore how a range (albeit a limited one) of language-learning MOOCs approach the teaching of language.

Question 2

How Can My ESL Students Best Use MOOCs?

We now look at how contemporary approaches to classroom and online language-learning interface with the affordances and constraints of MOOCs today. This section will also discuss referring students to xMOOCs or cMOOCs of any degree of interactivity to supplement their classroom language learning. First, with a content- or task-based ESL teaching orientation and some ESL teacher support, learners can take advantage of MOOCs that are not ostensibly created for the purpose of language teaching. Second, ESL teachers can also help students to select and make best use of MOOCs that do explicitly set out to teach language and communication skills.

Anderson's (2018) comprehensive study of first- and second-year college foreign language classes in the U.S. emphasizes how a **blended approach** (combining face-to-face classroom practices and online learning) permits teachers and their students to capitalize on an optimal combination of language-learning resources such as face-to-face tasks and activities, print and digital media, online chat, social media, discussion boards, self-paced tutorials, and games. Helping one's ESL learners take advantage of MOOCs is one such way to offer a richly textured blended learning experience to students.

ESL teachers can recommend that their students take a given MOOC to enhance their language learning, regardless of where it falls on the interactivity continuum, but more ESL teacher support may be required for those MOOCs that are less interactive. Whether a lecture-focused xMOOC, a particularly interactive xMOOC, or a cMOOC is chosen, an ESL teacher can help students optimize their use of MOOCs by offering coaching on how and why to take the MOOC. Romeo and Hubbard (2011) emphasize the positive impact of training learners on (1) **how to use** a technology, (2) **what to do** with it to address specific language-learning goals, and (3) **why** this use is valuable. These three elements are a helpful framework to think about when teachers refer students to MOOCs in a target language. This how-to-best-use-the-technology training improves learner capacity to use the resource more effectively and independently thereafter.

Content- and Task-Based ESL Learning in the MOOC Universe

The topics of MOOCs vary widely. Despite an early emphasis on computer science, in recent years MOOCs have emerged on every topic imaginable, from the emotional life of dogs, to acing a job interview, to particle physics, to identifying counterfeit food products. What should an ESL teacher consider when it comes to referring ESL students to MOOCs that are not explicitly designed for language learning?

Many readers of this book who teach ESL know that a popular approach in K-12 settings in the United States is **content-based** English language teaching. To be able to learn academic content, students need domain-specific vocabulary and awareness of domain-specific written and spoken genres of communication. A content approach to English language teaching can embrace a broad field, like biology, or more narrow academic subjects, such as botany or human anatomy. The idea of classroom-based ESL content instruction is that by scaffolding the vocabulary and grounding the reading, writing, speaking, and listening in the context of teaching academic content, students will be able to build up the linguistic resources and the requisite content background knowledge to be on par with their fluent English-speaking peers in that subject area in school. Referring one's students to existing MOOCs could be one component of exposing students to an academic context that uses language in authentic ways to explore that topic. The ESL teacher, however, may need to offer additional scaffolding of vocabulary and features of genres that students will need to read or watch in the MOOC, in order for participation in the MOOC to be accessible and useful to students.

Another approach promoted in many K-12 school districts is to expect the content-area classroom teacher to use inclusive pedagogies that scaffold the linguistic variety in the classroom and that supply the language needed to participate fully in the content class. In such settings there is often an ESL consultant who coaches content-area teachers in how to support their English language learners. Making MOOCs available to students as supplementary study materials and topic-focused language exposure could be part of what an ESL consultant could offer content-area teachers.

Any adolescent or adult learning a second language and needing to use that second language in a field of academics (EAP, or English for Academic Purposes) or work (ESP, or English for Specific Purposes, or Workplace English) may potentially benefit from participating in a MOOC in the target language on that specific academic or work domain. In this way, students can spend time with video lectures on the topic and can try to interact with other learners in the text-based discussion forums. The provision of content by video may provide (depending on the video style) visual support for concepts and enables students to review material multiple times and use subtitles to support their listening comprehension and the saliency of vocabulary.

Some MOOC videos feature crowdsourced translated subtitles in multiple languages. Despite the fact that a belief in 100 percent English immersion predominates in much of the U.S., ESL pedagogy research dating back to the 1990s (see for example Auerbach, 1993) indicates that dual language instruction may be more effective for academic development in both languages and in communication skills overall. Multilingual subtitles in content-oriented xMOOCs provide some small degree of multilingual access and validation of learners' multilingual resources.

An introductory MOOC on a given topic can also broaden a student's relevant content knowledge, a goal that may also be supported by multilingual subtitling of instructional videos. For this general-background purpose, a student might want to enroll in a broad survey course on a topic of interest. In contrast, participating in a focused, specialized MOOC can extend a learner's knowledge about a narrower topic. Students may wish to use MOOCs as part of pre-research for a class project or paper—a more multilayered and potentially more reliable resource than starting with Wikipedia. Since MOOCs are typically brief (3–6 weeks), they do often offer focused topics such as Stanford's course on the inner life of Dr. Martin Luther King, Jr., or the University of Rochester's course on understanding and performing the Blues, or the University of Toronto's course on the social context of mental health issues, which includes modules on the history of North American constructs around mental health and illness. In order to prepare for a project or paper in 1–2 weeks, a student could complete a focused MOOC more quickly, since MOOCs are usually **asynchronous** or self-paced. A student may need help from their ESL teacher locating an appropriate course if they are looking for something narrow. Some MOOCs only have a short run, so though a course may have been available one year, it may no longer be enrolling students the next.

Another way to support language learning in a content-focused MOOC is for learners to select a class on a topic they are already knowledgeable about, so that the space for learning involves matching known content to new language. For adults with a professional career background, this could mean taking a MOOC in one's professional domain. This approach is a good fit for ESP contexts such as English for nursing or English for accounting, where advanced students may be content-area specialists when the ESL teacher is sometimes not. Students could take, for example, the University of Colorado's "What Is Palliative Care?" (Coursera) beginner course in nursing, or the University of Virginia's "Financial Accounting Fundamentals" (Coursera), where the student would have already mastered the nursing or accounting content but needs to master communicating about that content in English.

In some cases, pointing students to participation in one element of a MOOC might be the most efficient approach. A computer programmer, for example, could take an "easy" programming MOOC and focus on the language used to talk about coding in both course videos and discussion forums. Personal expertise in a sport or hobby would equip a student to serve as a content-area expert in discussion forums, practicing the use of English to "talk" (in text) about a subject they are already well-versed in. Duke University's "Sports in Society" (Coursera) or the Museum of Modern Art's "Seeing through Photography" (Coursera) could be shown to students as examples.

The ESL teacher can guide their students in how to interact with such MOOCs to best effect. For example, if the challenge is vocabulary retrieval for impromptu speaking, the ESL teacher could guide their student to record oral summaries of lecture videos on their own phone. If pronunciation clarity is a challenge, students could play back a lecture video more slowly, and use the interactive transcript to repeat tricky chunks of speech, mirroring the audio. If use of stress and intonation could use work, a student could repeat short stretches of parts of lecture videos they really like, at reduced speed, using the interactive transcript to restart the video segment repeated, imagining that they are a voice actor trying to sound exactly like the voice of the original speaker. If students are going to take almost any future course in that field in the medium of English, they will likely be called upon to contribute to discussion forums online, so an ESL teacher could provide a rubric with which students could analyze the contributions of MOOC classmates to identify characteristics of discussion posts and to compose their own posts more effectively.

Taking a MOOC that is delivered in English on topics one is already an expert on could also mean taking a MOOC that offers an anglophone lens on a familiar culture one has grown up in or lived in. A student could take a course in English, for example, about the history or culture of their home country, such as Hanyang University's "Korea in a Global Context" (Coursera) or the University of British Columbia's "Chinese Thought: Ancient Wisdom Meets Modern Science" (Coursera), and assess the content of the course with a critical insider eye. A class of students working on writing could create a blog with reviews of MOOCs about different world cultures, practicing writing for an audience (other potential students) and practicing critical thinking skills and writing critiques. I would recommend scoping out what is available about cultures your students have lived in before proposing this idea to a student or a class, because there is uneven representation of global regions among social science and humanities MOOC courses.

In other words, approaching a MOOC for content-based language learning isn't limited to needing to learn that content. From each of these perspectives on taking advantage of content-based learning in MOOCs, the MOOC student can be learning target language vocabulary and usage and can participate in written and spoken genres of communication that are relevant to their English learning goals. In essence, while a MOOC that is teaching some bit of content is not ostensibly a language-learning MOOC, language learners can repurpose that MOOC to learn language to use in the contexts that matter to them.

Task-based learning is another popular approach in ESL school settings to teaching academic language. Groups of students need to collaborate to determine the steps needed to complete a task, to divvy out the roles, and to synthesize everyone's work together into a final product. In adult education settings, tasks tend to be real-world and practical, perhaps related to accomplishing something in the workplace or the community. One of the strengths of a task-based approach to language learning is that, due to the need to negotiate roles and agree on how to complete the task at each step along the way, there is ample practice of conversational routines for getting things done in teams.

Some MOOCs will lend themselves to a task-based approach, with assignments that require multiple steps and sometimes a degree of peer collaboration. A few MOOCs will actually assign group projects. Another way to harness the advantages of a group collaboration on a meaningful task is to organize a group of ESL students to take a MOOC together as a cohort and to meet either physically in person or live via videoconferencing to collaborate. The ESL teacher could provide support for online language-learning group work (Lee, 2016) that the MOOC may lack: establishing context, purpose, clear group instructions, support for negotiating group responsibilities, a transparent grading scheme, and a ready and engaged presence as students collaborate.

A particular kind of task used quite frequently in MOOCs is peer review, which often simply means assigning points to peer submissions in a rubric, and may sometimes involve written comments. Tasks that require human grading are often set up to be graded via rubric by peer review, and multiple peer review results are averaged. **Peer review**, as ESL teachers know, is something that English language learners are called upon to do in both formal school settings and in various ways in the workplace. Giving feedback to other people requires special language for politely making actionable suggestions and supplying specific praise. If these skills are part of an ESL teacher's curricular goals, many MOOCs supply a space in which learners can practice interpreting a rubric and supplying feedback comments. The MOOC will generally not do the heavy lifting of teaching students the language needed for these communicative functions, so the ESL teacher would still need to scaffold the process. In an advanced EAP setting, the ESL teacher might encourage learners to explore the norms regarding appropriate feedback established across different MOOCs and to critique the degree of transparency of these norms. Such an exercise could equip students to enhance their critical analysis of how they elect to communicate in a variety of online spaces.

Language-Learning MOOCs

Of course English language students can take an ESL MOOC in addition to exploiting content-based MOOCs for language learning. A growing number of MOOCs are dedicated to teaching language and communication, particularly grammar, academic writing, and business communication. Here we will look at popular theories about the optimal ways to teach a language online and measure language MOOC models against these theories.

The field of **CALL (computer-assisted language learning)** has long studied the particular advantages and challenges of online language learning in a variety of settings: solo and self-directed such as in the app *Duolingo*; in a group setting, such as an online semester-long course in a high school or university; and via social media and other forms of informal digital communication. A MOOC may involve any of these three modes of participation. As Meskill and Anthony (2015) explain in *Teaching Languages Online*, we now know a lot about how to implement online language learning so that it leads to successful outcomes. A subset of fundamental online language teaching practices can be well-served in most MOOCs: transparent learning objectives overall and for each task; consistent evaluation rubrics; strategic integration of authentic audio, video, and text; charging learners with a degree of responsibility; promoting a positive and welcoming climate; and promoting cooperation over competition among learners (Meskill & Anthony, 2015).

The asynchronous interactions typically built into MOOC discussion boards and peer review tasks supply extra time for learners to compose, refine, and practice language (Philp, Adams, and Iwashita, 2014). Well-crafted tasks can prompt students to take advantage of this time to attend to language form, to negotiate meaning, to reflect on usage, and to self-assess. The University of California system offers quite a few academic writing MOOCs, such as the "Getting Started with Essay Writing" from UC Irvine that includes a peer review task every week, and advice on how to give effective and supportive feedback. An ESL teacher referring students to a language MOOC can also point students to strategies that the asynchronous nature of MOOCs may help them use to best advantage.

xMOOCs as they are typically implemented, however, have difficulty supporting a second subset of the features of skilled online instruction. Meskill and Anthony (2015) underscore the critical role of the language teacher in online language learning. The skilled teacher adjusts the instructor contribution to each interaction in light of the context, the language production, and the goals of the learner and course. More specifically, this responsive interaction involves moment-to-moment adjustment of group formation, interaction, and tasks; locating and seizing teachable moments; sustaining a highly interactive instructor presence; and consistently tracking learner behavior, experience, and language production to optimize learning activities and interactions on an ongoing basis. Teacher responsiveness is motivational, turning an impersonal solo learning exercise into a collaborative community effort (Lawrence, 2017). To engage these factors in successful online language instruction, an ESL teacher could also enroll with their students as another student in a language MOOC if it had particularly valuable materials to offer, and thus responsively facilitate the learning experience of their own ESL students as a fellow participant.

As Meskill and Anthony (2015) point out, a special advantage of online environments is that they create traces of student language use in text, audio, and video that can be used for both **formative** and **summative assessment**. While a MOOC often creates big and interesting sets of data that researchers may examine to understand this learning context, reviewing records for formative assessment nonetheless would require a deeply involved teacher and a platform with adequate data-sharing policies. An ESL teacher participating as a student alongside their own ESL students would only have access to discussion board posts, possibly some assignments the ESL teacher could review as a "peer" reviewer, and communication with students outside the MOOC platform.

Language-learning xMOOCs often offer activities that are auto-gradable, rendering such exercises not particularly communicative. An eclectic communicative approach, nevertheless, also draws on older instructional strategies—such as form-focused grammar exercises, vocabulary translation lists or flashcards to memorize, and fill-in-the-blank sentences—all of which are straightforward to set up for machine grading. More specifically, structure-oriented grammar exercises can provide rehearsal of patterns or at least recognition of patterns. Vocabulary translation lists can contribute to the process of developing second-language vocabulary, though these lists generally lack insights about usage and context-dependent meanings. King's College, London, for example, launched "Basic English 1: Elementary" (FutureLearn) specifically as outreach to Arabic-speaking refugees in North Africa, and supplies an alphabetized list of vocabulary used in the course, translated into Arabic. Fill-in-the-blank sentences have the potential to trigger some noticing of collocational patterns in the language (words and phrases that tend to go together). When form-focused activities with "correct" answers are framed as opportunities to notice patterns in language, they can be particularly useful for adult and adolescent learners. Contemporary communicative pedagogical approaches tend to engage students in metacognitive consideration of why they are doing various activities and how each can further their linguistic knowledge and language skills. An ESL teacher referring students to a language MOOC could scaffold the experience by teaching students to approach form-focused activities reflectively.

One ongoing weakness of MOOC platforms for language learning is the lack of a mechanism for audio/video participation by learners. The few MOOCs that do integrate learner-generated audio or video require learners to use an alternate tool and paste a link or to use social media in addition to the MOOC platform. In other words, because most MOOC platforms constrain communication to text posts in discussion forums, a range of language use is precluded on the platform itself. Referring ESL teachers may wish to facilitate face-to-face or complementary online opportunities for conversation and discussion related to the MOOCs in which students are participating.

This overview has attempted to assist readers in selecting appropriate MOOC experiences to offer students. Notably, the role of the MOOC teacher is not listed in Table 1, which underscores the lack of live teacher presence in most MOOC provision. In my experience, teacher presence is strongest in the bigger MOOCs, in constructivist MOOCs, and in new MOOCs on their first or second run. Therefore, the referring ESL teacher bears the responsibility of scaffolding students' online learning experience to best advantage.

MOOC Learner Behaviors—A Language-Learning Asset or Curse?

Teachers, of course, can only guide learning behaviors, not control them. Any approach to language teaching relies on a set of beliefs about what learner behavior is likely to be. Thus, this is an additional factor to consider in referring one's ESL students to MOOCs.

Do learners in MOOCs behave differently from learners in more typical online courses or from learners in face-to-face classes? We know that in online classes, content and interactions need to be useful and engaging to sustain student participation. Online classes for school carry the penalty/reward of a grade, and for college often entail hefty tuition, both of which may boost participation. Online learning modules in a workplace are sometimes a requirement to do one's job, so this similarly prompts participation and completion in professional training online.

A MOOC generally lacks this penalty/reward structure. If you take (or "audit") a MOOC for free, there is no incentive to get your money's worth. In a large MOOC, the degree of student anonymity reduces the likelihood that students will feel bound to a social contract to show up for a teacher and classmates. Discussion threads with unmanageable subject lines and hundreds of serial posts can feel overwhelming and discourage students. In a small MOOC, the absence of this chaos may lead to a parallel discouragement, especially when there are not enough active students to complete assigned peer reviews. Given that there generally is no teacher interacting live with students, if participation by other students is minimal, students may feel alone and quit. Finally, many learners take a MOOC to explore an interest or to learn about something very specific that is one component of the course, so they may not be invested in completing the entire course, given their goals.

Given the absence of a traditional instructor, students are relatively anonymous in MOOCs. Anyone in the world may join the course for any reason, and platforms may reveal little to MOOC teachers about the students enrolled in their MOOCs. This anonymity adds another layer of distance between teacher and students. Contemporary language teachers are used to interacting directly with their students: seeing, hearing, and evaluating their language, for both offering feedback and formulating next steps in class. If students are motivated to participate by posting to discussion forums, MOOCs can nonetheless be a low-risk way to practice public-facing language, at least in writing, because of the degree of anonymity afforded by being one among thousands of learners in a popular course.

Exposure to and practice in using the target language in the MOOC setting is typically non-threatening and low stakes. Since most course content is provided through video, students can listen to content multiple times and view a transcript to support comprehension. A MOOC is also a low-risk participation context because, outside the formal educational system, participation is entirely voluntary. The behavior of students in the MOOC world reflects this optional nature. It is quite typical for students to participate in a self-introduction forum, watch a few videos, and be done.

There is a lot of angst among MOOC host institutions about non-completers and viewer-only students, given how we traditionally think about course-based learning. It can be distressing to see that, on average, across several major MOOC platforms, only up to five or ten percent of people who have signed up for a MOOC typically complete it (Kizilcec, Saltarelli, Reich, & Cohen, 2017; Jordan, 2014), but from another perspective, the MOOC landscape is one where tourists can poke around and stay or move on as they wish. MOOCs offer a different way of thinking about providing greater educational opportunities to potential students. In this way, MOOC behavior is more like informal, everyday-life, purpose-driven learning: I learn about something I need, or am interested in, until I've got what I need or until my attention shifts to something else. Therefore, MOOCs encourage learner autonomy in all its forms because sticking with a MOOC is dependent on learner motivation. Additionally, scheduling is controlled by the learner, as are focus and distraction.

MOOCs allow students to register and then explore a little, like browsing books at the library or shopping online, and then be done, potentially quite satisfied with what they have selected to pay attention to. Other students may choose to complete every assignment offered, watch all the course videos, participate in the forums, and dedicate time and attention regularly for a few weeks. A big proportion of learners sign up and then do not end up following through. Another large proportion of learners do the introductory activities and then hit a barrier, either internal or external to the course. Internal barriers may include an assignment for which one lacks the requisite knowledge, software, connection speed, or motivation. Some MOOCs offer a pre-test so that learners can find out if the class is likely to be a good fit, but this resource is not common. External barriers may include distraction, other demands on time, and competing priorities. Because MOOCs are so low stakes, there generally are no negative consequences to stepping away from a free, relatively anonymous online course.

What does all this mean for language learning?

- Teachers should encourage students to make conscious choices about how they want to structure and adhere to or abandon their involvement in any MOOC they have signed up for to improve their language and to feel empowered to do so.
- Teachers should be looking at other measures of success, grounded in research on effective language autonomous learning. (See, for example, Lai, 2017.) Teachers should be asking:
  - Are learners getting from the course what they are looking for?
  - Are students gaining access to extensive, authentic language input?
  - Are learners engaged in meaningful language use?
  - Are learners interacting and cooperating effectively with other students in the MOOC?
  - Are learners experiencing and contributing to a sense of community among students in the MOOC?
  - Do learners gain greater awareness about the target language, its use, or themselves as learners and communicators?
  - Are students critically reflecting on how and why they are participating in the MOOC in relation to language learning and language use?

  The answers to all of these questions may be yes even among MOOC non-completers. If so, then non-completion may not correlate with success as defined by learners.

Since MOOC teachers generally do not interact with enrolled students, the model is one of a teacherless mode of learning. For some courses, lower-paid course assistants monitor forums for problems, or even more proactively step into forums to summarize themes that emerge and to clarify takeaways. Language teaching without a teacher is an interesting conundrum. The lack of an interactive teacher presence in MOOCs is one reason that I strongly encourage ESL teachers to support and guide their own students in making the most of independent MOOC experiences.

Exploration 2: Find an Appropriate MOOC for Your Learners

In this exploration, shop around for a (free) MOOC that you could refer one group of your English language learners to. This might be a content MOOC or a language-learning MOOC. Class-Central.com is a useful resource, although it doesn't include all MOOCs on all platforms. You might check out these platforms to see if you find one that you think would serve your learners best:

Canvas Network
Coursera
EdX
FutureLearn
Udacity
You might also decide to select an alternate MOOC platform not on this list.

If this book were a MOOC, here I'd ask you to share what platform you picked and why, so that we could all learn from your insights. But for now at least, we're in an e-book, not a MOOC, so perhaps you will share your insights with other ESL teachers you know instead. You'll need to decide if you want to focus more on a content- or task-based course and guide your students to use that course to promote their language, or if you want to look for an actual English language course. Once you've picked a course, consider these important questions:

1. *How well does this MOOC align with your students' goals, skills, and needs?*
2. *Where there is a mismatch, what type of scaffolding could you provide to align the MOOC experience to your students' objectives and context more effectively?*
3. *How would you locate this MOOC in your instructional universe? Would participation be something done in class with your support? Homework? Optional? Required? Would you differentiate which MOOCs or which portions of the MOOC are assigned to different students or groups?*

Finally, if Exploration 2 doesn't suit your teaching context, how would you adapt it to make it work for you? This question invites you to practice scaffolding a MOOC for your students by considering how you might adjust this exercise to make it relevant for your own teaching context.

Question 3

What If I Am Asked to or Decide to Create a MOOC?

Institutions and teachers often launch MOOCs to meet a curricular or pre-curricular need or for public benefit. Also, a MOOC can promote an institution's more traditional offerings, whether face-to-face or online. Some MOOCs are created to build community among far-flung individuals with a common set of goals or interests. It's also important to state that MOOCs are typically not money-makers. Although some students pay for full access or pay for graded assignments or a certificate of completion, the majority of students access the free portions of MOOCs. But MOOCs may have the ability to bring money to institutions in other ways, such as recruiting students or garnering grant funding.

MOOCs are created by a wide range of educators. Most are affiliated with a university or educational testing or publishing firm, but if one has other resources for creating and assembling course materials, a range of platforms are available to host one's course for free. Canvas Network, for example, offers a MOOC for potential course creators called "Making MOOCs on a Budget" from the University of Technology in Sligo, Ireland. Language instructors in schools, nonprofit agencies, or private businesses may wish to share more broadly something that they are doing locally. School systems could use MOOCs as an inexpensive way to provide modular access to certain content, skills, or practice to any student in their learning community, such as how to take effective notes during a lecture, or how to study for an essay test. One could also involve one's students in creating a MOOC about the content they are learning or creating a new one-week module in an existing student-built MOOC. An educational provider may also be able to recruit new students by showcasing the quality of their programs with a MOOC.

The MOOC Creation Process

There are lots of ways to build a MOOC, but here we will talk about some of the most common paths. Perhaps one of these will be on your journey as an educator.

Who Teaches MOOCs?

Most MOOCs are taught by university-based instructors. Because some MOOC platforms are accessible to any creator, much like creating a YouTube channel, over time we are likely to see more MOOCs coming from teachers outside the university context and from non-academics with knowledge and advice to share. For now, however, making a MOOC typically requires a professional design and production team; most of these teams are located in universities or in university-related publishing and testing firms.

The host institution plays a significant role in getting a MOOC off the ground, ranging from funding the costs of creation and platform hosting to facilitating all elements of production. There are a few exceptions. I attended a live talk about MOOC-making from one of the co-creators of "Learning How to Learn," one of the world's early and most popular MOOCs, with thousands of students. Professor Barbara Oakley walked us through how she set up a home video studio and recorded and edited the filming of video lectures and animations largely independently. So it's possible, but, wow, that's a lot of work.

Institutional production is more common because it is generally very expensive to design and produce a new MOOC. First, instructional design teams collaborate with faculty to develop video and task content. Next, videographers and sound engineers record lectures, interviews, or other visual content in what are essentially television studios. These videos may then undergo significant editing, which takes time and leads to more costs. At the TESOL International Convention one year, I attended a talk about how the instructional design team at one university helps instructors create animations to illustrate concepts in their MOOC videos. This presenter, who had also been a language teacher, had moved into a full-time job as an instructional designer for language MOOCs on her campus. That degree of institutional support is not typical.

Importantly, while design and production teams are generally paid, it is rare for the teacher(s) initiating the course to be paid for design, for production, and for any follow-up attention to the course after it goes live, but teachers may be paid for their content and lectures.

Even with the critical work of the institutional production team, instructors of MOOCs still have an important role to play, in planning at least the curriculum and pedagogical approach. Instructors are involved in thinking through what students themselves will do in the MOOC and why. The same instructors involved in planning are often the stars of the show, the public-facing "talent" in the video production. A team of instructors is often involved in months of meetings to develop and refine course objectives, materials, and tasks.

What Should the MOOC's Curriculum Be?

As with most language curriculum design, the first step in contemplating making a new MOOC is to determine the learning objectives of the class. MOOCs, however, generally need to restrain the scope of objectives much more than traditional online, blended, or face-to-face semester-length courses. Objectives also need to be modular, because students may drop in for any part of the course, selecting a few menu items rather than consuming everything the course offers. Clear, narrow objectives allow for highly relevant learning activities and for broadcasting these clearly to potential students who are adding the MOOC to a full, busy life.

Unlike scaffolding participation in someone else's MOOC for students you have referred, when you create a MOOC, anyone may elect to take the course. One of the challenges for us at Michigan when planning our MOOC was predicting our student population. Who would find us? What might these students most want and need? What should drive the design of the course, the learning objectives, or a particular student audience? Often there is a bit of a dance between the topic of the course and the intended audience.

What are some practical ways to go about nailing down goals and anticipating your audience? Let's look at three examples. In the first, as Denise Comer (2014) details in "Learning how to teach . . . differently," she built course assignments carefully aligned to specific learning objectives to enable a vast and diverse array of learners to understand the course overall and the point of each activity. She reflected that this need for transparency enhanced her attention to communicating precise objectives in all of her teaching.

A second approach to creating a MOOC is to mirror an existing lecture-and-test-based course by recording lectures and reproducing tests online.

While quite common, this xMOOC reproduction approach delivers a version of what already exists to a larger audience, rather than assessing the needs and interests of the self-motivated, and huge, globally and linguistically diverse audience that MOOCs can attract.

In the third example, we created "Preparing for Graduate Study in the U.S." (Coursera) at the University of Michigan to address a need voiced by incoming international graduate students. Graduate school survey results of exiting Ph.D. students indicated that these scholars would have appreciated more language support early on. The director of my teaching unit proposed that we create a MOOC. To ensure that we were not reinventing the wheel, we searched a range of MOOC platforms, looking for something to fit the bill. Did a MOOC already exist that we could point our students to? We only found one MOOC on preparing for undergraduate life in the U.K., one on specialized health terminology for a narrow medical field in the U.S., and one on applying to U.S. undergraduate college programs. We thus decided that we should indeed create our own MOOC for prospective graduate students at any U.S. university based on what our students at Michigan reported they wished they'd had.

Our Story

Opting to base our course objectives on feedback from our own matriculated student population, we set about to brainstorm specific curriculum ideas with the ELT Editor/Director at our university press, who offered valuable insights and materials to use in the course. We drew up a list of goals that informal student input helped us refine. We identified two themes: forging one's public academic identity and building community. These thus became the two overarching themes of our new MOOC course.

We decided to focus on prompting and scaffolding the use of the English language to address these goals. We picked an "elevator pitch," or brief self-introduction, as the capstone project for the course and as the focus of repeated language practice. In this way, students could be preparing for a speaking task that they would be called upon to repeat in real life on a daily basis the first few weeks of every term: introducing themselves to faculty, administrators, peers, students, and community members in a manner that would establish their professional identity and credibility, also fostering interpersonal connections.

Once we had a tentative set of course goals, a final project, and a syllabus laid out, it was time to propose the MOOC to our college. The course was approved, which released an array of support from our Academic Innovation office, the home for MOOCs on our campus. We were assigned a design team with deep experience in online learning, curriculum design, and project management. We met regularly as a group to determine exactly how to translate our vision for the course into the MOOC world. The many conversations about who the course was for, what the course hoped to achieve, and how to get there shaped the MOOC that came to be. I composed scripts for short videos to introduce each of the five units in the course. I then worked with a talented videographer and video editor to create these brief videos. These videos differed from a more typical xMOOC, where video-recorded lectures deliver the lion's share of content in a course. Here, the one- to three-minute "lectures" were designed as a frame for each course theme that students would elaborate content in response to. The short "lecture" videos were also a means to enhance students' sense of teacher social presence in the class. I also scripted two tutorial video "screencasts" to show students how to use two online corpora (MICASE and MICUSP) that feature academic language use. Perhaps most importantly, I identified extant YouTube video footage of graduate students talking about graduate life and sought permission to embed clips I selected from these videos in the course. After taking the course, students reported to me that they found these videos particularly compelling.

I was lucky to be able to pilot the course design in a small, private online course setting, by offering the course online to 30 incoming Michigan graduate students before it went live as a MOOC. My department also contracted with our university's teaching center to complete a comprehensive evaluation of the pilot course in terms of student experience and first-semester outcomes. I used this experience and feedback to adjust the MOOC course design, reducing the number of activities, making some activities optional, and revising and re-recording the brief video introductions to each unit.

To communicate these curricular plans across the production team, we created a spreadsheet with one row for each activity in the class. Columns included the objectives of each activity, the activity type for each (e.g., streamed video, in-video questions, reading, discussion forum, quiz, post a link to a video, peer review), text instructions for each activity, links to media files, and auto-response items for quiz-based tutorials. Then, we were ready to turn this grid over to a team of course builders to translate the spreadsheet and video files into live activities in the Coursera MOOC.

If only the process were so simple. Our MOOC sought to promote greater language awareness and fluency by designing the course within a communicative and constructivist approach. In other words, we wanted to foster language development and context exploration, rather than providing extensive information, even though the teacher role would be extremely limited. We bumped up against the constraints of various MOOC platforms pretty quickly. Discussion forums were quite linear, with limited ways to search and display posts, and without opportunities for tagging. Students couldn't embed video or audio. In our case, we had wanted to provide students ample opportunity to speak.

We had initially planned to host live online meet-ups of small student groups around shared tasks, but this proved to be too ambitious given our limited active staff resources and all the variation in global participant schedules. Video chat rooms did not work because students would be participating asynchronously, on different days and from different time zones all over the world. We eventually decided to ask students to post their videos online on YouTube or elsewhere and to supply a link in designated discussion forums. This wasn't ideal for stimulating a lot of peer viewing, but we compensated for that by setting up peer review activities to encourage and support responses to classmates' videos. Throughout this process of responding to platform constraints, we updated the detailed spreadsheet of learning activities.

An alumnus of our small, local pilot of the course served as a talented troubleshooter and responsive problem-solver in the first year of the MOOC. This helped to get the community off the ground. This was a paid position (5 to 10 hours a week), a resource the course was again lucky to have. Once our MOOC reached an enrollment of about 3,000 students, we had a critical mass for the course to operate more successfully without such active moderation by a course assistant, and newer MOOC students started relying more on one another and earlier discussion forum posts for help, community, and motivation. Moderating the course is still critical to resolving issues that come up, but it is less needed to shepherd students through the course once a student body reaches critical mass. How long it takes to reach critical mass and how critical mass is defined will depend on many factors, including course objectives, degree of interactivity, and even marketing of the course by the institution or platform.

Seven MOOC Design Tips

Based on my first MOOC creation experience, here are seven tips if you're thinking about building a language MOOC.

Tip #1: Assess Student Needs and Define Learning Outcomes

Clearly establishing specific course objectives is a key component of any solid course design, but how do you do this when a wide variety of students will self-register for any number of reasons? Is this okay? Is a needs assessment targeted at one small group of students you know about enough? This is the reality: You build it, and you don't really know who will come. Nonetheless, like any online "product," such as mobile apps or software, you can do some market analysis and pilot testing to get a pretty good sense of your potential audience and to gather some initial feedback. Invest time in communicating (via text and video) what outcomes students can expect through participation in your course. As your MOOC completes a few cycles, student participation can guide future revisions.

Tip #2: Determine the Level of Staffing Needed and Available

Determine what active staffing is needed and available to plan the course, build the course, launch the course, and then to troubleshoot and interact with students. A Duke University report on Duke's first Coursera course in 2013 details the more than 600 hours spent on planning, building, and implementation (Belanger & Thornton, 2013). Designating a person to keep an eye on discussion forums for frustrated students or golden "teaching moment" opportunities is a valuable investment in getting a new course rolling. Identify any resources possible to recruit, hire, and supervise a teaching assistant who could closely monitor the course, including the following possible responsibilities:

- Monitor discussion boards for students seeking help; triage help requests, which might include things like:
  - pointing students to the platform's tech support
  - identifying community behavior problems (e.g., using disparaging language toward other students) and issuing warnings or restricting participation
  - prompting student peers to step in to try answering content questions
  - clarifying task instructions
  - providing encouraging feedback
- Notify the course instructor about
  - repeated concerns
  - opportunities to clarify tasks

  - broken links
  - evidence of learning success
- Provide peer review when a lack of required peer reviewers is preventing an active student from continuing to participate.

Explore other ways to create "teacher presence," such as short videos and personal anecdotes from the teacher(s) threaded through the course. Live "office hours" on a social media or videoconferencing platform are another popular way to add drop-in teacher presence, but it is tricky to assemble students from across the globe at the same time. Some courses record Q&As with faculty stemming from common discussion forum questions in one cohort and then subsequently make this video permanently available to future cohorts.

Tip #3: Plan for Materials

There are several aspects of materials to consider when building a MOOC, in addition to what one would typically plan for in a traditional online course. First, because a MOOC operates in the public sphere, and thus publishes content to a potentially unlimited audience, course creators need to obtain permission to use any copyrighted materials (print, video, or other media), to select public domain materials, or to create new materials. Second, keep videos and readings brief. Check with your institutional design team on length norms on the platforms available to you. Third, plan for reusable video materials. You will probably want to renovate your course periodically. It is likely that there will be versions 2.0 and 3.0 of a new MOOC. There is so much time invested in video development, production, and editing that it may be too costly to make adjustments to video footage with the same frequency as other course materials. It can be a long-term timesaver to keep video segments independent from specific assignment instructions and date references. Fourth, if video materials will be used to teach content, plan for more than talking heads. Consider images, demonstrations, footage of authentic communication, animations, and screencasts. Finally, do not be intimidated by the idea of creating quizzes or tests. Even without expertise as a test item-writer, you can use the quiz tool as a means of helping students see whether what they understand, know, or can do matches your expectations. You can populate a quiz tool with rich feedback, and treat quizzes more like tutorials than assessments.

Tip #4: Decide on Any Culminating Activities

Final wrap-up activities may drive the early practice activities threaded throughout the course. In our case, for example, we built up to the final "elevator pitch" assignment by asking students to introduce themselves (by supplying a link to a video), to write out and peer review a possible script for an elevator pitch, to discuss what they bring to the table, and to analyze a sample elevator pitch. Quiz-based tutorials also invited students to examine language used in elevator pitches.

Tip #5: Create Two Collaborative Planning Documents

Create a course overview that the entire development and instructional team can reference. Keep this overview at a macro level so that all involved can see the learning objectives and trajectory of the course. Also create a detailed course roadmap document (I like using Google Sheets spreadsheets for the course roadmap because multiple team members can collaborate online at any time). The roadmap should list, at a minimum, the following information about every item that students will view or do:

- item name
- item type
- relevant learning objectives
- script or outline (if a video)
- task instructions (if an assignment)
- questions/prompts and automated feedback (if a quiz)
- links to relevant files or sites or apps
- status
- completion deadline
- person(s) responsible
- notes. Notes may include peculiarities of a given task, or information about permissions to use copyrighted material, for example.

Tip # 6: Designate a Final Reviewer for the Content and Tasks

If you can recruit someone else to go through the content and to follow the instructions for each task, such a trial run can help to sort out potential confusion before the course goes live. This was tremendously valuable for our

MOOC. If your course was authored by a team, the reviewer could also offer editorial suggestions to maintain a consistent authorial voice.

Tip #7: Review the Feasibility of Your Plans Given Timeline Constraints

As I've emphasized, creating, building, and implementing a MOOC is a complex process involving a team of contributors, usually from multiple departments in one or more institutions. Double (or maybe triple) the time you expect everything to take. Since MOOC development work is time-intensive and compensation for development will vary by institution, consider realistically how much time weekly can be reserved for this purpose.

Rolling It Out

To move from design to implementation, it's necessary to pick your platform, to build out your course on that platform (hopefully with a team of talented helpers), to do some beta testing and then, after launch, to set up ways to feed, nurture, and replenish your MOOC.

While MOOC platforms have some features in common—such as streaming video content, a quiz tool, a discussion tool, a course navigation system, and the capacity to handle thousands of learners—they also have differences in emphasis and flexibility. Given how quickly the feature set changes (even during the process of designing a course for a specific platform), I won't try to characterize specific MOOC platforms here. Instead, I'll offer a list of elements to consider if you are contemplating which platform to use to develop a new MOOC.

- Make a list of the ways that you'd like students to interact with
  - the course material
  - other students
  - the instructor(s)
  - the digital and analog world outside the MOOC.

  These will help you to analyze which platform(s) will require the fewest compromises.

- How much data about students and their work will be available to you, the teacher? How easy or hard is it to get this data? For example, can you see how many students respond to a given prompt or can you view text responses to an open-ended quiz item?

- How easy is it to get into the course system to repair quick-fix problems, such as clarifying task instructions, once the course goes live?
- How much flexibility do you have with the look and feel, such as color palette, sequencing of content, institutional branding, or embedding of third-party apps?
- What are your responsibilities to the platform? How do you report the alignment between course tasks or modules and course objectives? Is there a review process that your videos, content, and syllabus need to pass through? If so, how does that work, and will it be useful to you and to your course?
- Who "owns" your course and your materials after launch? What are your options for using third-party materials with written permission?
- What privacy considerations does the platform offer your students? How does a "right to be forgotten" (see European Union GDPR law) work on the platform?
- What are your options and opportunities for communicating with your learners, should you wish to do so?
- Which components of the course (if any) can students access without paying? What components can students be required to pay for?
- What proportion of student payment will be paid to you, if any? Is there a cost recovery threshold the course must reach first?

After selecting the platform, making any revisions to course design due to the constraints and affordances of that platform, and building out the course on that platform, it is useful to conduct even informal beta testing. **Beta testing** simply means that you have what you think is a final draft of the course ready to go, and you involve some volunteers as students to test it out and see how it works. Through their involvement and potentially their feedback, you can identify gaps in task instructions, technical items that don't quite work as planned, or content issues. The graduate student who was going to serve as our course assistant worked through each activity in the course to test it out and to provide important feedback. He became keenly aware of the student experience in the course before we started enrolling students, which helped him to be an even more effective course assistant. If beta testing is not possible, some courses use the first month of launch as a beta-testing period, then make minor adjustments as needed.

A/B testing is another mechanism for comparing two versions of an activity or lesson on some MOOC platforms. The A/B feature allows a single MOOC or a task within a MOOC to have two versions, where students are randomly assigned to one or the other but are unaware there is an alternate version. Then the instructor(s), designers, and host institution can obtain comparative data about student participation, performance, or persistence in each group.

Finally, the MOOC does need some care and attention after it goes live, particularly during the first few months as it gathers steam. MOOC teachers or institutional teams can recruit former students, in-service teachers, or graduate or undergraduate students as discussion board monitors. Our first course assistant was instrumental in the successful experience of students in the MOOC in its first year. He kept a close eye on discussion forums and shout-outs for help from enrolled students. When some students didn't collect enough peer reviews, he provided the missing peer reviews. He offered wise feedback on how we might adjust the course going forward. Some institutions have a budget to pay course assistants. Some of this funding comes from the fees MOOC students pay for long-term access, course certificates, or other MOOC credentials. Some course assistants are volunteers, often recruited from the pool of course alumni. The sponsoring institution, not the MOOC platform, is generally responsible for recruiting assistants, setting up moderator access for assistants, supervising assistants, and handling any payment or volunteer recognition.

The next step in nurturing the MOOC, after the first few months, is to contemplate adjustments to the syllabus and to tweak course objectives to match what real students are looking for, just as in a typical face-to-face course. Depending on the goals and audience for your course, this review might be conducted annually. After implementing any major changes, it would make sense to observe student behavior closely for a couple of cohorts to be sure that changes are working as planned.

So overall, while MOOCs are usually designed for minimal live teacher involvement, keeping a MOOC going generally means continuing to involve someone who is paying attention to how the course is going, how students are faring, and how the course could be improved in later iterations. If you're putting together a MOOC without a large design and implementation team to help you, be sure to plan time over the subsequent months and even years to nurture your MOOC as it grows.

Exploration 3: If You Could Plan a MOOC . . .

In this final exploration, contemplate a need that one group of your English language students has that your current curriculum doesn't adequately address and that you want to provide additional support for. What possible type of practice, content, or skill would benefit these students? Can you find support for that practice, content, or skill already existing in the MOOC world? If not, what might be possible to build in your instructional context? What resources are available to you? How would you ideally want to handle access (accessibility, connectivity, and what students have to pay for) and privacy? Who could you collaborate with in your institution and professional networks?

Epilogue

What's on the MOOC Language-Learning Horizon?

What's next in the MOOC world, especially for language learning? MOOC design teams are exploring new reasons for offering MOOCs, and platform design researchers are exploring new uses of technology.

What are some of these new types of courses? The University of Michigan, for example, has been experimenting with "teach-outs," modeled after the campus teach-ins of half a century ago. Each brief (1–2 day) teach-out focuses on a contemporary problem and engages participants in exploring that problem and how to solve it. A number of institutions are using MOOC platforms to provide pre-arrival disciplinary orientations to large numbers of incoming traditional students. Others are designing MOOCs for actual university course credit. There have not been a lot of forays into secondary education yet, but I anticipate that as online instruction grows for young teens, more teen-focused MOOCs will emerge. It will be important for language educators to help guide quality and to engage teens themselves in determining how MOOCs 2.0 or 3.0 should be designed.

As technology advances, we can also anticipate technological innovations in MOOCs. Adaptive learning, which provides a differentiated experience based on learner performance, is facilitated by emerging "machine learning" technology. MOOCs may become a space for research and exploration of machine learning applications because of the vast number of students possible in any given MOOC, and machine learning's reliance on large data sets. As audio and video interfaces for interacting with digital technology become more ubiquitous, we should finally begin to see tools that enable meaningful oral communication among participants in MOOC-based language courses, perhaps even without a consistently involved instructor.

In the meantime, as emphasized here, we have an opportunity as ESL teachers to help our students plug in to what MOOCs can offer today: a supplementary space in which to develop vocabulary and text-based conversational skills and to learn foundational content in domains of interest at an individual pace in a non-threatening, low-stakes environment.

REFERENCES

Anderson, H. M. (2018). *Blended basic language courses: Design, pedagogy, and implementation.* New York: Routledge.

Auerbach, E. (1993). Re-examining English only in the ESL classroom. *TESOL Quarterly, 27*(1), 9–32.

Belanger, Y., & Thornton, J. (2013). *Bioelectricity: A quantitative approach: Duke University's first MOOC.* [Internal report.] Retrieved from https://dukespace.lib.duke.edu/dspace/bitstream/handle/10161/6216/Duke_Bioelectricity_MOOC_Fall2012.pdf

Comer, D. (2014). Learning how to teach... differently: Extracts from a MOOC instructor's journal. In S. D. Krause & C. Lowe (Eds.), *Invasion of the MOOCs: The promise and perils of massive open online courses* (pp. 130–149). Anderson, SC: Parlor Press.

Freire, P. (1970). *Pedagogy of the oppressed.* New York: Herder and Herder.

Gardner, D., & Miller, L. (2014). *Managing self-access language learning.* Hong Kong: City University of Hong Kong Press.

Jordan, K. (2014). Initial trends in enrolment and completion of massive open online courses. *The International Review of Research in Open and Distributed Learning, 15*(1). Retrieved from http://www.irrodl.org/index.php/irrodl/article/view/1651/2774

Kizilcec, R. F., Saltarelli, A. J., Reich, J., & Cohen, G. L. (2017). Closing global achievement gaps in MOOCs: Brief interventions address social identity threat at scale. *Science, 355*(6322). doi: 11.126/science.aag2063

Lai, C. (2017). *Autonomous language learning with technology: Beyond the classroom.* London: Bloomsbury Academic.

Lawrence, G. (2017). Integrating the "human feel" into online second/additional language teaching approaches. In J. B. Cummings & M. L. Blatherwick (Eds.), *Creative dimensions of teaching and learning in the 21st century* (pp. 139–149). Rotterdam, The Netherlands: Sense Publishers. doi 10.1007/978-94-6351-047-9_13

Lee, L. (2016). Autonomous learning through task-based instruction in fully online language courses. *Language Learning & Technology, 20*(2), 81–97. Retrieved from http://llt.msu.edu/issues/june2016/lee.pdf

Lewin, T. (2012). Instruction for masses knocks down campus walls. *New York Times*, March 4. http://www.nytimes.com

Meskill, C., & Anthony, N. (2015). *Teaching languages online.* Bristol, UK: Multilingual Matters.

Murphy, L. (2015). Online language teaching: The learner's perspective. In R. Hampel & U. Stickler (Eds.), *Developing online language teaching* (pp. 45–62). New York: Palgrave Macmillan.

Philp, J., Adams, R., & Iwashita, N. (2014). *Peer interaction and second language learning.* New York: Routledge.

Romeo, K., & Hubbard, P. (2011). Pervasive CALL learner training for improving listening proficiency. In M. Levy, F. Blin, C. Bradin Siskin, & O. Takeuchi (Eds.), *WorldCALL International perspectives on computer-assisted language learning* (pp. 215–229). New York: Routledge.

Vygotsky, L. S. (1978). *Mind in society: The development of higher psychological processes.* Cambridge, MA: Harvard University Press.

Yeager, C., Hurley-Dasgupta, B., & Bliss, C. A. (2013). cMOOCs and global learning: An authentic alternative. *Journal of Asynchronous Learning Networks, 17*(2), 113–147. Retrieved from ERIC database.